FLY CASTING

with **BILL CAIRNS**

Photography by HANSON CARROLL

STONE WALL PRESS · LEXINGTON · MASSACHUSETTS

Contents

Fly Fishing
The Most Versatile Method

The history of fly fishing is one of gradual evolution in both equipment and method. From crude beginnings small refinements appeared periodically to gain ultimate acceptance and become absorbed into everyday usage. This has been the case for hundreds of years and certainly is the continuing case today as fly fishing expands rapidly in popularity and, in fact, spills over into areas where it was never considered a factor before.

Traditionally, fly fishing has had a venerable association with the trout and salmon angler. Then, too, it has been a method rather commonly employed by the fisherman seeking the various panfish, bass and pike. In the last several years we have witnessed a dramatic and effective increase in the use of the fly rod in salt water. What we have now is an angling method of unusual versatility and potential. Under the right conditions anything from a six inch trout to a six foot tarpon is within our range of effectiveness.

The equipment manufacturers of today have become increasingly aware of and responsive to these expanding demands. Every equipment component we use reflects improvement over what was formerly available, even a few short years ago.

There are fly rods on hand to meet the requirements of delicacy when dealing with a shy trout on a midge-feeding kick, rods that will boom a bass bug into a stiff breeze, or rods with the power and backbone to lever a salt water streamer ahead of the malevolent eye of a striped bass. The modern fly lines are a far cry from the "silk only" tapers of my early years. There is a variety of line taper types, weight and densities that will equip us well for surface or subsurface activity. Fly reels are comparatively light in weight, simple and sturdy in design, and reliable in use. Monofilament has matured to fill the need for reliable and consistent leader materials. Also, its characteristics permit us to build more functional leader tapers than has ever been the case before.

7

Atlantic Salmon, *Tabusintac River, New Brunswick.*

Although there can be no question that today's fly fisherman may express himself in a variety of ways, it would be incorrect to label fly fishing as ideally suited to every situation that may be encountered. Each method available, be it live bait, spinning or baitcasting has something to offer because at one time or another it meets a definite need due to specific conditions. Yet for most species on a comparative basis, the fly rod offers more potential—more of the time.

Consider that virtually every inland sport fish we might seek is a consumer of various insect, crustacean and forage fish forms. These food forms constitute the bulk of their day to day diet. No method except fly fishing can hope to simulate these forms as well under so many varying regional and seasonal conditions. Whether the food of the moment is a mayfly or midge, ant or shrimp, caddis larva or stonefly nymph, grasshopper or baitfish matters little. All these and more are easily within the scope of the fly rodder to imitate artfully and present in a realistic manner.

In some quarters fly fishing has been regarded as extremely difficult and requiring a truly consummate skill.

This isn't the case at all. The pure mechanics of fly casting can be learned in a relatively short time. It is obvious there is much more to fly fishing than just fly casting. The more knowledge acquired about the habits and preferences of what you intend to fish for, the more potential for success exists. However, to translate such knowledge into something meaningful, you must have a reasonable competence with the fly rod.

The casting fundamentals should become so well ingrained that you are not really conscious of them. You spot the intended target, the rod raises instinctively, the backcast unrolls to tug nicely against the rod, the rod moves forward. Line, leader and fly unroll to drop— just where they should.

When this point is reached you will enjoy fly fishing to the fullest. Then as your further involvement with the sport grows, I'm sure you will regard fly fishing as the complete sport.

Fly fishing has many benefits. It can occupy us both physically and mentally. It is a sport enjoyable by one's self, or still more enjoyable when shared with companions. The sport can be played close to home. True, around metropolitan areas there may not be any fine trout streams, but a little looking will turn up overlooked panfish and bass potential. Or, if you live near the coastline there are many

Brown Trout, *Chimehuin River, Argentina.*

superb opportunities to exploit. Of course if circumstances permit, you can travel the ends of the earth in search of fly rod trophies only to find, "you should have been here" (a) last week, (b) last month or (c) next week. Fly fishing may lead to spin-off hobbies or interests such as fly tying or the further study of stream life. It is the most democratic of sports. Young or old, man or woman—it matters not a whit to the fish. And the fish is always the variable, the unknown. Some days are extremely productive, other days our best efforts result in few, if any, strikes. It is a sport where we can catch and release the fish to enjoy another day's sport. Finally, no other sport has the heritage of literature that fly fishing offers.

All of these facets combine to make fly fishing not a mysterious specialty for a select few, but rather a complete sport that will prove to be the most interesting, challenging, versatile and productive of them all.

Random Thoughts on Fly Casting

The problems of fly casting are related to but somewhat different from those encountered in bait-casting or spinning. In these other casting forms the lure, speeding forward, pulls out the following line.

Fly casting is less efficient. The fly is virtually weightless so it cannot contribute to the casting cycle. The true burden of casting weight is in the fly line, distributed over several feet.

In effect a spin lure makes the ride possible, a fly simply goes along for the ride.

Having the effective casting weight concentrated in a small spin lure as opposed to having the weight spread over several feet makes a difference in the manner by which we handle the equipment factors.

In spinning the lure is brought close to the rod tip, a quick "wristy" backward swing can properly load the rod and we can instantly flip the lure forward. This same motion, if applied to fly casting strokes would be awkward, tiring and inefficient.

The fly casting strokes are of necessity much longer. The fact that the casting weight is distributed over many feet slows down the whole cycle. The fly caster typically will pick up several feet of extended line with a smoothly accelerating up and back motion, pause briefly to permit the line to straighten out behind, then the rod pushes down and forward. The fly line moves forward in a loop which gradually straightens to fully extend the line, leader and fly and drop gently to the water.

The fly caster pulls and pushes an extended line weight—an important difference from other casting forms.

All this makes it sound as though fly casters will exhibit cookie-cutter conformity in style. This isn't the case at all. In watching a number of fine fly casters it is apparent there is no single correct style. There are, however, fundamentals which each in his own way will adhere to. I would liken the situation to an individual's handwriting. Presumably all of us learned similar fundamentals of pen-

Accelerating into the Backcast.

manship away back in grade school. Over a period of time an individual style emerged. As long as the end result of our penmanship is reasonably legible, then the purpose is served.

Over a period of time this analogy has come to express my opinion on various fly casting styles. There are what I believe to be fundamental points of reference, but once these fundamentals are under

12

control there will always be the emergence of an individual style. Unconsciously we will gravitate to whatever seems most natural to us as individual casters. A few of the obvious variables between people that will exert an influence are timing, coordination and physique.

The novice caster must realize that fly casting is an acquired skill, not an instinctive ability. Each fine caster has spent a good deal of

The Forward Loop is formed.

Use the full arm.

time in mastering his craft. Yet, as we progress through the various casts you'll come to realize there are only a few moves that must be made correctly. Literally anyone who can tie his shoes without tipping over can and will learn to cast a rather good line.

The modern fundamentals of casting are quite different than those passed out when I was half a fly rod high. The old instruction manuals advised keeping the elbow close to the body. Indeed, it was good form to clamp a book between elbow and body and cast without dropping the book into the brook. This style spawned a group of wrist casters as the wrist became the pivot point of the entire cast.

14

This was an adequate, if tiring, style for short line work. But now we regard this elbow close to the body style as obsolete. Equipment improvements as well as the expansion of fly fishing into new areas of expression where long line techniques are vital are among the contributing factors for this change of style.

Furthermore, any wrist-casting style makes its greatest demands on the comparatively small muscle groups of the hand and wrist. These tend to tire quickly. As they do the casting suffers correspondingly.

Today we utilize the entire arm with the elbow as the pivot point of the cast and much less wrist action. Basically the forearm, wrist and hand become an extension of the rod throughout most of the cast. Pivoting off the elbow utilizes the larger muscle groups of the arm and shoulder. The stresses of the casting motions are better absorbed and distributed. The results in modern casting being both more effective and less tiring.

Although fly casting is not difficult, it will be advantageous if you can arrange for regular practice sessions. In each practice session think through every move that you make, consciously trying to make each cast better than the last one.

If you simply swish the rod back and forth without this conscious effort, incorrect habit patterns will be established that will prove difficult to break.

With proper attention to detail and regular practice sessions you will soon establish a correct pattern of muscle memory. Fly casting will become completely natural and comfortable.

Rigging Up

With the rod assembled and the reel in place, most fly-rodders will then take the fine leader end and begin to pass it through each of of the line guides. About halfway through this process and, as often as not, the leader slips away from your grasp to slide back through the guides and pile up on the lawn.

The easiest way to rig up is to start with the rod butt resting on the ground, pull off about 20′ of the fly line. Then, a few feet back from the end of the line, double it over and pass this doubled line through each of the guides. You will both see it and feel it more easily. Also, if you do happen to let go, the line tends to hang in the guides rather than sliding all the way back through them.

Rest butt of the pole on the ground and pass the doubled line through each of the guides.

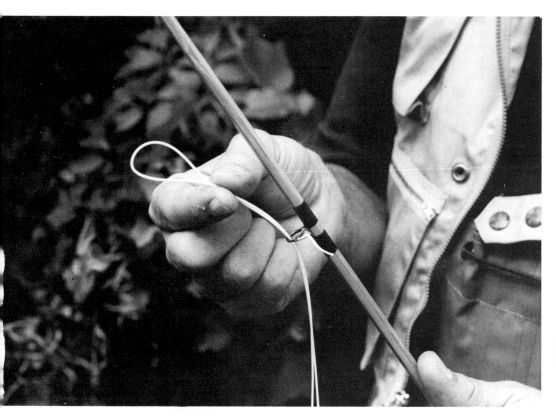

Doubling the line makes rod rigging easy.

17

Getting Ready to Cast

The Grip

There are several potential ways to grip the rod, but the most effective and comfortable is to press the thumb on top of the grip, centering the corks.

The applied pressure of the grip is best described as comfortably firm. If the grip is too loose, chances are the entire casting cycle will be underpowered. If a "stranglehold" grip is maintained, it will prove very tiring and soon cause a cramped feeling in the hand, wrist and forearm.

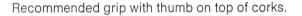

Recommended grip with thumb on top of corks.

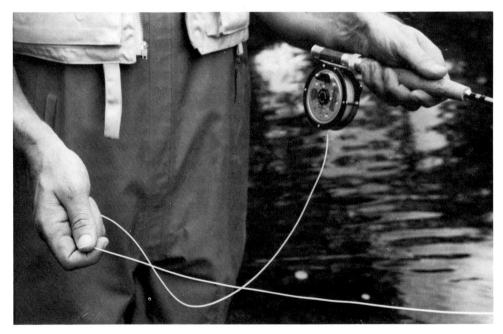

Alternative grip, thumb to the side.

There are two other grips that are often employed. Some casters prefer to have the thumb to the side of the corks, rather than on top. This grip has sometimes been referred to as the *free wrist* style. There can be no question that the wrist does have greater flexibility from this position. Frankly, this potential for the wrist to bend is the reason I advise the new caster against it. One of the most common hurdles to overcome is a slack wrist at the top of the backcast. With the thumb to the side the potential to drop the rod too far backwards is too great. The experienced caster with a thorough knowledge of the fundamentals can utilize this grip style most effectively.

The other oft-seen grip utilizes the forefinger extended along the top of the corks. Advocates of this style maintain that the forefinger guiding the rod provides great accuracy to the cast. Yet, it is no more effective in this instance than the thumb on top style. This grip is often used by casters employing lightweight, short rods. Many rods in this category have undersized grips to keep overall weight factors to a minimum. The thumb extended along the grip isn't as comfort-

Alternative grip, extended forefinger on top.

able as the extended forefinger. I find when using rods with such undersized grips that I'm constantly shifting between placing the thumb on top and extending the forefinger on top. If from this you might deduce that I'm not a fancier of such tiny grips, you would be totally correct.

The real drawback of the forefinger grip comes when you are handling larger, more powerful rods. This grip style just isn't as strong.

In all fairness to advocates of this style, I must mention that one of the finest casters I know uses this grip exclusively. I've watched him push powerful nine foot rods around New Brunswick salmon rivers under the most adverse conditions, all with apparent ease.

The Arm Position

For average-length casts the upper arm is naturally and comfortably at the side, the elbow is slightly separated from the body. The forearm, wrist (which is bent down slightly) and hand (with the thumb on top) point straight down the rod and extended line.

The pickup from the water will be made with the elbow pivot, the hand, wrist and forearm remaining a stiffish continuation of the rod butt. The thrust is in an up and back motion, accelerating smoothly. As the rod approaches vertical there is an upward "kick" and immediate stop to the wrist motion. The feeling in hand is as though you were trying to throw the line directly overhead. It won't go directly overhead, of course, because the momentum imparted to the line is both up and back—that is the path the line will take.

Proper arm, hand, and wrist positions.

With the rod stopped at the top of the backcast, you will find it angled upwards and somewhat past the vertical.

There is a slight pause at this point for the line to unroll to the rear; then the arm reverses the original path by moving down and forward. At the moment of turnover the wrist comes into play once again to emphasize the forward stroke. The rod is stopped slightly above parallel.

The basic arm motion can operate from any angle. Moving the rod along a horizontal path gives us an ability to cast under low-lying shrubs or perhaps to work various curve casts. Bringing the rod backhand across the body may compensate for crosswind factors or being hemmed in on the rod side by obstacles.

The point is that there is a basic arm motion. Although the norm is to operate overhead, you can cast from any angle.

Collapsing the rod too far back will ground the Backcast.

The Stance

The basic requirement is that the stance be comfortable and natural. If you are right-handed the normal stance will have you facing the target, the right foot slightly behind the left. The body weight is distributed mostly on the right foot. Also, it will be advantageous to open up the right foot slightly. The reason for opening the stance in this manner is to enable you to turn your head and watch the formation of the backcast. You will in time become sensitive to the line weight tugging slightly to the rear and know instinctively when to start forward. But this is an elusive feel in the beginning. Turning to watch the backcast will help you acquire the proper timing that much sooner.

Opening the stance permits the caster to follow the path of the Backcast.

Recommended stance; left handers would, of course, reverse foot positions.

Some instructors favor a different starting point entirely. The right-handed caster would stand facing the direction of the cast squarely with the right foot in advance of the left. Most of the body weight would favor the right foot. This position restricts the ability of the caster to turn and watch the backcast; so I recommend the originally described position as most natural and appropriate.

Alternative stance.

In short order you won't be conscious of the stance anyway. Once the fundamentals of casting are acquired you'll be working from every conceivable position, whether it is seated in a raft floating the Snake or balanced precariously on a midstream rock. If you see a casting target such as a rising fish, you'll get the rod in motion to cover it.

The Basic Cast

Fly casting can be practiced on the lawn as well as on the stream. If you have not cast at all before and will be working on the grass, an open area of about fifty feet will suffice to start with. Lay the outfit on the lawn and walk off about twenty feet of line. If your first session is on the stream, turn to face downriver and strip off the same twenty feet of line and feed it to the current. It will soon straighten out below you.

Recall that it is the fly line that is our casting weight. If only a few feet of line extend beyond the rod tip, there will be insufficient weight to properly flex the rod. If too much line extends beyond the rod tip, it will be awkward and difficult to manage smoothly.

To acquire the feel of the equipment and the basic motions involved, only the rod hand should be used initially. You do not want additional line creeping off the reel at this point so hold the line to the cork grip with the rod hand. In other words, the line lies in the palm of the hand as you grip the fly rod with the same hand.

The grip on the rod is comfortably firm with the thumb on top of the corks. The upper arm is close to the body, the elbow is separated from the body a comfortable couple of inches, the forearm and rod point right down the line. Thus the rod is about parallel to the lawn. The stance is comfortable, the rod-side foot sustaining most of the body weight and it is opened slightly to permit you to watch the unrolling backcast.

Begin the backcast motion with a smooth, firm, steady lift—pivoting off the elbow and keeping the wrist stiff. The motion is upward and backward, accelerating quickly and smoothly. As the rod approaches vertical there is the slightest pickup with the wrist to emphasize the height of the backcast. Tightening the thumb and forefinger as this wrist "kick" is made will stop the rod at the proper angle. At the top of the backcast your thumb is pointed straight up, the rod is angled up and back of the true vertical.

You should be turning your head to watch the upward thrust of the backcast. Now, there is a slight pause to permit the line to straighten in the air behind you. Your clue in watching the line is just as the backcast begins to drop from its high elevation you begin the forward stroke. This timing is critical to casting ease. If you don't pause long enough for the line to extend itself, there will be a loud "whip-crack" sound. If the pause is overly long, the backcast will collapse and fall to the ground behind you.

Assuming you've made the correct timing pause and the backcast properly straightens, the forward cast is almost automatic. Just reverse the path of the arm and rod. The forearm, hand and wrist are stiff, pushing down and forward and accelerating progressively. As the turnover of the rod begins, tighten the thumb and forefinger, squeeze, and bring the wrist into play. Then—STOP. The rod is aimed slightly above the parallel. This lets the line loop extend fully; the leader and fly straighten themselves out, and everything falls gently to the surface.

Repeat the procedure several times. Don't hurry! Be sure to make each cast a complete cycle. That is, don't simply swish the rod back and forth. Let each cast extend fully and drop to the lawn. Then, try again, carefully thinking each move through and consciously trying to make each cast better than the last.

In all our normal work the rod does most of the job; we guide it smoothly into the proper position by making the proper moves.

New casting hands tend to minimize the importance of the backcast, putting all the emphasis into the forward stroke. This is dead wrong! If the backcast is formed correctly the forward stroke virtually takes care of itself. Remember it takes as much, perhaps more effort to lift into a good backcast. Coming forward we have gravity assisting us. Be sure to pay the greatest amount of attention to forming a neat, smooth backcast.

Remember, too, that the wrist is stiff throughout most, but not all of the sequence. Be careful of the wrist motion at the top of the backcast—the danger is too much motion, dropping the rod parallel to the grass in back which grounds the backcast. The wrist motion emphasizes the height and speed of the unrolling backcast and puts your hand in position where it is ready to start the forward stroke. At the turnover of the rod in front, the wrist again emphasizes the final delivery.

The Fishing Cast

Under actual fishing conditions both hands will constantly be utilized. One hand controls the rod movements, the other hand holds and controls the line.

Understandably the novice caster pays almost total attention to the rod hand only and ignores the role of the line holding hand. Yet, even fundamental fly casting is a two-handed job. As distance needs increase, the role of the line hand becomes even more important. Ignoring the importance of the line hand will make it impossible to achieve complete mastery of the equipment.

All fly casting steps can and should be learned in a progressive

Proper position of the hands at the start of the normal fishing cast.

Lifting into the Backcast, line hand anchors the cast.

manner. Each new step that is introduced is built on a previously acquired fundamental. Let's see then why I emphasize the role of the line hand.

If we take a typical caster waving the rod back and forth and keeping the line holding hand stationary what happens is this . . . the rod lifts up and back, the line hand is perhaps at a waist high position and stationary. Now, as the backcast unrolls the fly line is slightly shortened across the body which may cause a premature grounding of

Left, Line hand moves to maintain tension. Right, At the completion of the cast, line hand opens to let "shoot" extend cast.

the backcast. Then as the rod moves forward it is essentially sliding up the line and a bulge of slack develops between the first guide and the line hand at the critical moment of rod turnover. This power loss dissipates the energy of the forward stroke and a floppy line loop forms. There was slack line when there should have been tension.

Form the habit now . . . of moving the line hand with the rod. This habit is essential to rapid progress as a fly caster. From this fundamental of both hands working together we'll gain the ability to shoot

29

line easily for extra distance, compensate instantaneously for the sudden vagaries of the wind, increase our accuracy and lead us logically into single and double haul techniques.

If there is a single major fault of the average caster it is in not fully understanding the role of the line hand and its contribution to effortless fly casting.

In our basic fishing cast the rod hand will be doing exactly as before. Strip off three or four feet of line from the reel. Grasp it between thumb and forefinger a comfortable distance apart from the rod. As the rod lifts into the backcast the line holding hand simply moves up and across the body, maintaining the original distance between rod hand and line hand. A constant tension is exerted on the line and the two components of the cast, the rod and the line are moving and working in complete unison. There is no line speed variance or power loss. Coming down and into the forward stroke we simply reverse the path of both rod hand and line hand. At the moment of rod turnover we can release the line from the line-holding hand. It will funnel out through the guides and add a couple extra feet to the cast. This slight "shoot" is always desirable as it helps cushion the final line extension and assure a gentle delivery of the fly.

If there is a specific spot you've chosen to deliver the fly to, this line-holding hand contributes to your accuracy. Cast with a bit more power than is needed to reach the target. Instead of just letting go with the line hand at the final shoot, open the fingers slightly so the line flows easily through them. Clamping the fingers together just slightly can slow the line in the air, and pinching them together will stop the further flow of line and drop the fly—just precisely where you want it to be.

The single problem is the timing of the release from the line holding hand. If you release line prematurely there hasn't been time for the loop to unroll far enough to develop its own pulling capability. If you release too late, the loop has already gone by and cannot pick up the weight of the slack line and carry a shoot. Therefore you should work on the smooth timing . . . at the moment of rod turnover, open the hand to make the slack available. It will be carried out in the normal course of the extending forward cast.

Once the timing is mastered you'll be making long and effortless shoots of line for extra distance. But always stress timing and rhythm. With these, distance is going to be a natural progression.

Side view, line is lifting into the Backcast.

Backcast unrolls high and to the rear.

Rod swings forward. The loop forms and will straighten over the water.

Rear view, Backcast unrolls high and to the rear.

Forward Stroke begins—arm drops down and forward.

Loop is formed and will extend to drop the fly gently.

36

From the other side. Backcast lies flat out to the rear.

Both hands contribute to the Forward Stroke.

Forward Cast is stopped, line "takes off" and extra line is released
from line-hand.

False Cast

By now you have been working with the rod long enough so that it is no longer necessary to strip line off the reel and walk it out. Instead you can use the false cast. Strip the same amount of line off the reel and flip it into the air. Working the rod back and forth you can extend the line. False casting will serve other functions as well on the stream.

It will dry the fly between deliveries, it can be used to accurately measure the distance you wish to cast and false casting can also serve to work the line around to a new direction.

Let's take a quick look at these specifics. You'll see the virtues and need for false casting cycles. The dry fly should, of course, float on the surface of the water. However, the fly will pick up water droplets as it rides the waves. A couple of false cast motions "shake" them off, drying the fly and assuring a proper, perky float when it is returned in the next cast. A known location such as a rising trout should be covered with some accuracy; the false casting cycle lines you up with regard to distance and direction. Finally, you may be working up and down the stream in a normal casting sequence when you spot a fish off to the side. From a fully extended backcast you can pivot at the hips and drive the rod in the new direction with great accuracy. If it is a radical change of degrees, a couple of false casts can work you around a bit at a time.

The false cast is, in effect, an incomplete cast. The backcast is made in a normal manner but the forward stroke is stopped with the rod butt angling about 45 degrees above the horizontal. You pause long enough here to allow the line to extend fully—in the air—then move into another backcast motion. As a rule, two or three false casting cycles will serve any purpose; then the fly should be delivered to the water in the usual completion of the cast.

Excessive false casting, indulged in by so many anglers, serves no valid purpose and may prove to be self defeating. The longer the line is in the air the more potential for timing errors or dropped backcasts to occur. Avoid the tendency to simply false cast back and forth repeatedly unless there is a valid reason to do so.

Although the illusion of false casting is that both backward and forward strokes are made in the same plane, the truth is the cycle is a very narrow oval. The backcast comes up with a slightly circular up and back path, the forward cast in a vertical plane. This will minimize the tendency of the line to tangle with the rod during the casting cycle.

False Cast has been stopped on the Forward Stroke. Tilt rod to the outside and come back and up.

Roll Cast

Many stream sections have a foliage or rock barrier marching to the river's edge that prevents a normal backcast motion. Still, a forward line extension is needed to fish the water effectively.

The answer lies in the roll cast. Although execution is not difficult, many an angler has by-passed the virtues of the roll. It is, however, the single cast that requires water in a practice session. The tension of the line on the water makes it all possible. This tension is lacking on the grass and the line simply slides ineffectually. There is one way to get the principle on grass—if you round up a willing partner. Have

Rod is lifting very slowly to draw the line into proper position prior to Roll Cast.

Rod is stopped. Line loop is forming outside the elbow.

your partner stand on the leader. This anchors the cast. You can make the roll motions work; then your partner's problem is ducking out of the way as the advancing loop threatens to strangle him. But that's his problem, not yours—right?

A fundamental requirement of any cast is to get the line in a position where the rod can effectively push against the line weight. This is, of course, usually achieved by the backcast in our normal strokes. What we do in the roll cast then to achieve this goal is to tilt the rod slightly away from the body. Elevate the rod slowly until your hand is in the same position it would occupy in the pause position at the top of a backcast—this is with the hand about opposite the ear. A belly of line will now form outside and slightly behind the rod arm elbow. Stop here, just as you would pause between the backcast and the forward cast in a normal stroke. This stop is essential. Completion of the cast is identical to the forward stroke of any cast. The arm pushes down and forward. The line begins to move

43

forward before the leader and line leave the surface. The advancing loop picks leader and fly off and extends them straight out in front of you.

In restricted quarters or with strong gusty sidewinds, this cast (like any other) can be done in a backhand motion. Elevate the rod across the body, tilting it away, allow the loop to form, stop briefly and then push down and across the front of the body.

Forward Stroke begins. Rod arm pushes down and forward.

Extend arm straight ahead.

Line is released from line-holding hand to add distance.

Backhand roll is also easily handled.

Drive arm and hand down across the body and forward.

Steeple Cast

To some degree the steeple cast may be considered an occasional alternative to the roll cast. When the foliage hems us in closely, the roll cast is likely to be the better choice. Yet there may simply be low-lying trees or shrubs to the rear, a bit too high to be comfortably handled with a normal lift and backcast, but of a height that could be easily cleared by the steeple cast. As the name implies we're literally throwing the line straight up. Barely pausing, we immediately come forward. By not allowing the normal pause between strokes we minimize the possibility of the line falling down into the obstacle behind us.

The execution of the cast is an exaggerated full arm thrust— straight up. Drop the arm down and forward almost immediately. From this fully extended, high arm position it is quite easy to slap the surface too vigorously with the forward cast. Basically you have the force of gravity assisting you on the forward stroke; so you are almost guiding the line into the forward cast.

The steeple cast can be very effective at short and medium distances. As the length requirements of the forward stroke get longer and longer, execution is more difficult due to altitude of the backcast. If you really have to reach out from confined quarters, look to the roll cast rather than the steeple cast.

Steeple Cast is an upward jerky thrust.　　　　49

Side Casts
Curve Casts

Vern Bressler led me through the Wyoming meadow to a network of crystal clear spring creeks. Before he headed downstream, he cautioned that these fish were easily spooked in the alcohol clear water. Forewarned, I moved cautiously upstream to the confluence of a tiny feeder into the main spring creek. From a kneeling position I peeked over the meadow grass and there, where the currents converged, were eight cutthroats from 2 to 4 pounds swaying easily in the slow flow.

Picking out the nearest fish I started a normal overhead stroke and before the cast could straighten each of the fish flushed for parts unknown. The high rod angle and sudden movement were obvious to the critical fish. It was also apparent that after several days on the big water I'd gotten careless. For the remainder of the day the name of the game was to maintain a low profile and work side casts. This side cast does offer the virtue of a much lower rod angle, and on many streams it will become a stock in trade over choosy fish.

The side cast also permits modifications in timing that will let us throw curves. There are valuable techniques hidden in the horizontal move.

In general a natural free float of the fly is the desired result of the cast. Oftentimes though, the current is quicker where the fly line lies than where the fly lands. The larger diameter fly line is caused to move rapidly on the water and soon pulls the fly in an unnatural manner.

This drag is most unattractive to suspicious fish, and for all practical purposes it has been a wasted cast. Worse yet, the commotion of the dragging fly may well put a wary fish down temporarily.

The initial answer to handling such conflicting currents lies in throwing a curve. The curve comes in for other applications as well. A fish lying ahead of an obstacle might be unapproachable from any angle but below. The cast that hooks in around the obstacle can often

Side Arm Cast is basis of curve casts.

Negative curve is underpowered.

make the difference. It makes the best presentation of the desired fly possible.

Vermont's Lamoille River hadn't been kind to me that hot July day. Normally productive runs and riffles were void of any taking fish. A leisurely walk along the stream bank finally brought me to a deep, slow-flowing pool. More to cool off than anything else I entered the tail of the pool. Both banks were overhung with alders and the center of the pool was very deep. Along the right hand bank looking upstream I saw a quiet dimple beneath the overhanging shrubs. The depth of the pool in midstream was too great to allow me to position more nearly opposite the rise as I would have preferred. The single possibility was an upstream curve bending the fly in under the alder sweeps. The rod set in motion and the little ant tucked in beneath the overhangs and drifted to the willing and waiting fish. Once in a while it all goes together right.

52

Positive curve is overpowered. Throw the tip in vigorously.

The next couple hours were spent in a slow stalk of individual risers. Wading to position and getting the curves right was a tedious business. There was nothing memorable about either the size or numbers of the fish, but I look back on that day as a most satisfying one.

The easiest way to throw these curves is to operate from the side. You will recall that our basic cast can come from any angle and no matter what the point of origin is. If it is a well-timed delivery, the result is a straight line. Recognizing this, we see that if we cast side-arm the line loops form roughly parallel to the water and a properly timed cast will straighten out in front of us. But an underpowered side cast will fail to attain the straight line; it will fall in a negative curve. Conversely, an overpowered side cast will extend the leader and fly past the straight line and result in a positive curve.

The negative curve is probably the easiest to start with. In fact, with a short line just underpower your usual side cast stroke and you'll see the principal very quickly.

If the cast is straightening out, too much power is being applied. It may take several tries to hit it right since the unconscious tendency is to try and throw a normal straightline extension. What you are trying to accomplish is a premature arrival of the line on the water. This takes very little power to achieve.

At longer casting distances loop or hold several feet of excess slack in the line hand. Make a horizontal pickup and backcast. Keep the motions slightly underpowered using the middle of the rod without any final tip-action input. After the backcast straightens, bring the rod forward again, slightly underpowered, using the middle of the rod without the usual thumb and wrist pressure acceleration. Before the line loop straightens, release the slack from the line-holding hand. This premature release of the slack stops the loop from completing itself and straightening out. Properly done, the line falls in a negative curve on the water.

In effect, this negative curve is the opposite of everything we normally try to do. It is an incomplete, underpowered cast in every respect.

To some degree the amount of potential curve is controlled by the rod angle when casting. The true sidearm cast can throw the deepest curve. A higher rod angle permits less of a curve.

The positive curve differs in execution in that we shall overpower the cast. The side cast is again used as the basis of the cast's formation. Start with the horizontal pickup and backcast using unnatural motion with the final wrist and thumb impetus to keep a neat, narrow loop. After the backcast straightens start the forward stroke with more power than would be needed to simply straighten the line. Finish with a forceful wrist and thumb pressure application. A short line hand pull just as the thumb pressure is applied will help "throw the tip in." At the finish of the cast stop the rod abruptly and raise the rod tip slightly. This overpowered motion will cause the leader and fly to swing past their normal straight line. The leader and fly will turn into a positive curve on the water.

Curves can also be done easily with backhand casting strokes. This can be valuable if you're hemmed in on the casting arm side by foliage. A lazy backhand cast will make the negative curve, a forceful backhand cast, aided by the line hand tug, will kick into a positive curve.

Mending the Line

Although the use of curve casts may permit the line, leader and fly to fall correctly on the water, they cannot assure the continued natural drift that is desirable.

Casting across a quick current to drift the fly in the adjacent slower flow still means the line caught in the rapid section will be moved quickly. Unless some compensation for the variable current speeds is made, the current will soon belly the line and cause inevitable drag.

Mending the line will restore the desired natural drift anytime drag threatens. In this instance an upstream mend would be made. To execute the mend, hold the rod in front and roll the forearm, hand and wrist in an upstream direction. This "flipping" of the tip will pick line off the surface and roll it back upstream.

Depending on the complexity of the currents, it may be necessary to make several mends in a single cast.

Avoid overpowering the mending motions. It is only the line in danger of immediate drag that you're concerned with. If the motion is too vigorous, it will cause undue movement to the fly by itself.

After a short time you'll be reading the currents well and be able to anticipate when drag may occur. Automatically you will make the compensation. Also, it is well to anticipate in order to allow the fly to ride naturally over a specific spot. For instance, you may have selected a particular area where you feel there is a chance of taking a fish. The cast has been made well above the target site to permit the fly to drift naturally over the fish. If there appears to be the possibility of drag taking hold when the fly is over the fish, you want to make the mend before hand. Then if the mend had been a bit too vigorous and disturbed the drifting fly, it has occurred well above the taking lie where the fish probably did not notice and become alarmed. This foresight also assures the fly drifting correctly in the critical area of the fish's position.

Flip tip with rolling motion of the forearm, wrist, and hand. The line follows the energy impulse and rolls over to restore natural float.

It is also possible to cast a mend in the air. As the forward cast starts to unroll, simply flip the rod tip upstream or downstream, whichever will be needed. The shooting line, still to flow out of the guides, will bend into a curve and drop that way on the water.

The very deep turbulent streams often harbor big trout which must be worked at a bottom-bouncing level. For this we often use a sinking fly line. The sinking line is a devil to mend—once it has had a chance to sink deep. The usual technique is to cast across the stream and make a full arm, vigorous upstream mend just as the cast settles on the water. This slack lets the fly get deep quickly and tends to keep the fly sideways to upstream looking fish. This broadside float means the fly is in its most visible position with relation to the fish. Then simply follow the continuing downstream path of the fly with the rod tip. Pay particular attention as the fly comes under tension, downstream and across from you. Fish often choose that moment to strike.

In shallow water a sinktip line will be ideal. The sinking portion lets your fly work at the correct level; the floating running line is easy to mend if it's called for.

Slack Line Casts

A slack line or "S" shaped cast can often be utilized to advantage. In dry fly work when there are conflicting current flows, one of these casts may effectively retard drag. Also, cross stream or even directly downstream casts may benefit by one of these moves to hinder drag effects and extend a natural float.

The S cast takes advantage of the fundamental that whatever is done to the rod during the cast will be reflected a moment later in the flow of the line. The procedure is to make a normal pickup and backcast, allowing it to straighten to the rear in the customary manner. Then, as the rod moves into the forward stroke it is wiggled from side to side. The thumb stays uppermost on the cork grip throughout this cast. The line passing through the guides follows the side to side motions of the rod and will extend to drop on the water in a series of curves or S's.

You will find it possible to exercise a great deal of control over the number and size of the curves that are formed. A few widely spaced wiggles of the rod will produce a few deep curves; a rapid pulsating series of short side to side motions will drop a large number of small curves.

There are alternate ways of dropping a slack line cast as well. In the first alternative the pickup and backcast are made in the normal manner, but you will cast forward with greater emphasis than is required to reach your desired distance. At the end of the forward cast, pull back slightly on the rod. This "pullback" is a short motion of only a few inches. The abrupt stop to the speeding line will cause it to bounce back and fall in a loose series of curves.

Another method to accomplish much the same result is often termed the *parachute cast*. Essentially it involves an incomplete forward cast. Work out the desired amount of fly line in a normal false-casting cycle. On the final forward delivery, start the rod straight

The "S" cast will drop a series of curves to the water.

ahead, then stop it abruptly while it is still in a vertical position. That is, do not follow through the forward stroke. Your rod hand will have moved from a position about opposite your ear straight ahead for about eighteen inches and then stopped. Immediately lower the rod hand about a foot. This incomplete forward stroke will yank the line and leader backward. As the rod is lowered from its vertical position, the line will fall loosely to the water.

Shooting More Line

As a general rule we customarily shoot a foot or two of slack line with each cast to cushion the arrival of the fly to the water. This assures a gentle delivery.

It is possible, with proper timing, to extend this line shoot for several more feet. The key to success is timing the release of the slack line from the line hand.

Strip off some six or eight feet of line from the reel and hold this excess in a few loose coils with the line hand. Make the usual back-cast and forward stroke. Immediately after you have applied the final

The usual release permits a short "shoot" to cushion the arrival of the fly.

wrist and thumb emphasis to the forward cast, open the line hand to permit the loose coils to spiral out through the guides. The developing pulling weight of the line speeding forward beyond the rod tip will tug this "shooting line" out for added yardage.

You must recognize it is only the pulling weight of the line beyond the rod tip that can overcome the weight and inertia of the slack line and tug it out through the guides. If you release the slack from the line hand too soon or too late, an extra bonus of distance is impossible. In essence, all you do is make the slack available for the pulling fly line beyond the tip to yank this along on its flight.

Although this action will suffice for ordinary work, you still may need to make an almost instantaneous longer shoot to reach a distant fish or to compensate for a sudden gust of wind. Then it will be a case of "pulling in" more line speed. The inherent advantage of both hands working together now becomes obvious. With the line always under control there is split second compensation available.

We have stressed that the line hand always follows the moving rod, maintaining more or less constant tension on the line. We know, therefore, that as we move the rod up into a normal backcast position the line hand is moving also. At the pause position at the top of the backcast, the rod hand is about opposite the ear, the line hand is about at chest height, and there is tension on the line.

From this positioning we can shoot a considerable amount of line by single hauling. Start the forward cast smoothly and forcefully, at the same time the line holding hand pulls smoothly and quickly down and back to about a hip pocket position. From this position the line can be immediately released. The resultant increase in line speed will carry a fly for much extra yardage or drill it into a gusty breeze.

The single haul is a natural progression from our basic concept of both hands being valuable in every cast. It also leads directly into easier mastery of the true long distance technique—*the double haul.*

Both hands drive forward.

The Double Haul

The cast with the greatest distance potential of them all is the double haul. Although this is the case in which it will be imperative to keep smoothness and timing in mind as the real keys to success. The capable caster always works in phase with his equipment; he never tries to simply overpower it.

Since you will be handling more motions in the double haul, it is advisable to start practice with more than the usual amount of line extended beyond the rod tip.

Lay out about thirty-five feet of line as a starting point. If you want to shoot additional amounts of line, you can strip it off the reel and either hold it in large, loose coils, or allow it to drop at your feet.

Lean forward slightly from the waist. Your grip on the rod is a bit firmer than usual (you will be handling longer line lengths than usual), and the line hand reaches toward the first or butt guide to grip the line between thumb and forefinger.

Most casters start a line hand pull a split second before the rod begins to lift. This gets the line moving towards the caster and assists in powering into a smooth, fast backcast. Both hands then work in opposing directions—the rod hand moves powerfully up and back, the line hand is sweeping smoothly down and back, heading for a hip pocket position. The hands are greatly separated at this point. As the backcast unrolls to the rear, the line hand (still holding the line in the same relative place) moves up across the body towards the reel. With the backcast straight out behind the rod, the line hand starts a smooth acceleration back towards the hip pocket position. The rod drives straight ahead and a forceful wrist and thumb delivery complete the turnover of the rod.

If the one cycle wasn't enough to gain the desired distance or the timing wasn't quite precise, it is a simple matter to false cast a time or two and then release for the final shoot.

Double haul country of wind, big water and big fish.

Many anglers look on the double haul as only required by big water anglers. To be sure it is a valuable big water technique, but the fundamentals can be employed with any tackle (even the lightest) to advantage. On small water just a slight tug of the line hand breaks surface tension and moves a line into a smooth riding backcast, a tiny pull coming forward can shoot a line for extra yardage or compensate for a puff of wind.

In brief, the double haul is valuable for any fly rodder whether it is the task of the day to kick a bass bug into a narrow pocket or to lay a long line over distant fish.

The double haul can be done with the double taper or weight forward line, but many anglers who habitually must reach way out are using the so-called shooting head. This is a short (usually twenty-two to thirty-two feet) section of line, attached either to one hundred feet of 20 to 25 lb. monofilament, or a specially made level fly line .029 in diameter. Then conventional backing line fills out the balance of the reel spool. Anglers working with the shooting heads have devised some unique methods of handling the loose running line behind the "head." Some have rigged paper clips or clothespins to their wader tops on which to hand the coils. Some have held the loose coils between their lips and on the forward shoot they open their mouth (hopefully) to let it soar. More and more are converting to the specially designed shooting basket to handle the retrieved line. It certainly does simplify life! The recovered line is simply stripped into the basket attached at the waist and then shot from it on the subsequent forward stroke. By implication, the use of a shooting head means handling a long line rather continuously with the double haul as the basic cast. If you use a shooting head for the first time, there are a couple of items you will quickly become aware of in order to obtain the best results.

Keep the shooting head beyond, but close to, the rod tip when casting. If the head is too far from the rod tip, the light monofilament or level fly line may not be able to support it properly. Grounded backcasts may occur. This overhang or distance from rod tip to the end of the actual shooting head should be one to three feet as a starting point.

On the final forward stroke, aim and release well above the parallel. You aim higher than you would with the usual double taper or weight forward line. Otherwise there may be line tangles on the outgoing flight of the taper.

Reach forward with line hand, maintain a firm rod hand grip.

Both hands are in motion. Line hand pulling down and back, rod hand moving up into forceful backcast.

Line holding hand drifts up towards the reel.

Line hand pulls smoothly down. Rod drives ahead.

Left, both hands continue. Line hand heading. For hip pocket position—rod moving ahead for final ''turnover.'' *Right,* wrist and thumb emphasize the forward stroke. The line is released to shoot through the guides.

If not enough speed has been generated in one complete haul, you can false cast to build up additional speed.

The arm can "drift" back with the extending back cast. Line hand is drifting towards the reel.

Forceful forward drive of the rod combines with sweeping line hand pull. Line will be released from this point.

The stripping or shooting basket simplifies handling of excess shooting line.

Retrieved line can be dropped into the basket.

Coping with the Wind

The wind is an obvious fact of an angler's life. It may whistle out of any compass point and no matter from whence it originates, if it is strong enough, it must be compensated for.

Novice hands automatically assume that the wind blowing from directly behind the caster is beneficial. In the case of a gentle breeze, perhaps this is so, but if the tailwinds are strong a few trial casts will quickly revise your thinking.

With a strong tailwind you move back into the normal backcast and find it is strongly retarded by the wind. That now familiar feeling of the line weight snuggling against the rod is missing. There is no sense of proper rhythm and control. The first few casts may simply collapse in a wind-blown heap. This is especially true if you are trying to handle a long line on the backcast.

There are various methods of dealing with the wind that whistles from the rear. Depending on the velocities you are dealing with, you will find one of the following compensations satisfactory.

The usual approach to tailwinds consists of making a short forceful backcast with about twenty to twenty-five feet of line. Usually this movement into the backcast is assisted by a smoothline hand pull on the pickup to gain extra speed. The wind will buffet the backcast down (near the water) then a forward stroke is aimed high—well above the parallel. If a long forward cast is required, another line hand haul is in order. Aiming the cast high in a rather open loop will give the following wind the ability to soar it for a long flight.

This method works quite nicely as a rule except that there is often a brief moment when the wind is in control, not the man behind the rod. This occurs when the backcast rides up and is apt to be blown around by the wind. My preference if the tailwinds are really howling is to start with the rod held low and in front. Then make a forceful horizontal pickup aided by a short, smooth line hand haul. The rod angles are essentially the same as you would employ in the usual side or curve cast. This keeps the line moving low where it may be less affected by the wind. The line loop forms parallel with the water, rather than being buffeted down by the wind.

Turn your head to watch the unrolling of the loop. As it straightens to the rear, immediately start a looping overhand forward stroke. There is no pause in the whole cycle. The forward stroke is aimed high to take whatever advantage you can of the following gusts. The loops of the backcast and the forward cast are widely separated, therefore there is no danger of them tangling. The line weight nestles continuously against the rod so you have greater control. Again, it is important not to allow the usual pause at the end of the backcast. It is one smooth, continuous oval motion which starts to the side and sweeps up and overhead.

There is yet another alternative that offers possibilities. Just turn around and face into the wind. Make a strong hauling cast into the teeth of the breeze; then loft a strong high backcast and follow it by rotating at the hips and releasing the backcast to ride with the wind.

The wind that faces the caster really presents only a problem of its velocity. You will have no trouble in obtaining a smooth high back-cast, so the key to defeating headwinds lies in the smooth accelerating velocity you can impart to the forward stroke. Remember always that timing and smoothness are more important than strength. Facing a headwind is no exception. Many casters faced with such winds try to overpower the equipment and lose all sense of coordination. As a rule you will find the double haul technique most helpful in giving you extra line speed against oncoming breezes. The only difference is you will want to delay for as long as possible the final turnover of the rod into the wind. You want to throw a tight, narrow loop so there is a minimum of line surface for the wind to buffet about. Drive the rod well forward and keep it low to the water while smoothly giving a line hand pull.

The crosswinds seem, on the whole, to cause more problems for casters than any other. This is understandable since the weight factors involved in fly casting are minimal and a gusty crosswind can cause a real problem. I once saw an angler decorated with a big Gray Ghost streamer fly in the side of his neck because he ignored the blustery winds that swept the stream.

The ideal is obvious enough: the rod should always be on the downwind side. If, for example, you are right handed and the wind is gusting from left to right there is no problem. However if the wind is crossing from right to left there is the potential for the line and fly to whistle in dangerously close to your head or body.

As usual there are a few compensations that are possible and your choice may depend on the strength of the winds at any given time. A strong sidecast will be sufficient for slight breezes; the velocity of the moving line will be enough so that it isn't blown too close to you. Stronger winds call for different measures. One possibility is to slightly alter the casting planes. If you are right handed, make the backcast with the rod tilted away slightly to the right and keep the rod hand quite high as the backcast unrolls to the rear. Then as you come forward, alter the plane of the forward stroke. Bring your hand virtually overhead, the line will be riding high and will pass to your left.

The final compensation may be the best and safest of all for severe crossing winds. This is the *backhand cast.* The execution of the cast is not difficult. Start by holding the rod in the usual manner (thumb on top) but pointing to the downwind side. That is, if you are right handed and the wind is blowing from right to left you are angling the rod across your body and to the left. The pickup is made off the elbow, assisted by a short line hand tug and the rod angles up over your left shoulder. The backcast unrolls safely downwind and you are ready for the forward stroke. This moves ahead with the usual stiffish forearm drive, assisted by the ending wrist and thumb emphasis. A smooth line hand tug on the forward cast will give extra speed and distance to the forward cast if it's needed.

All of these wind compensations should be practiced from time to time. Not only are they handy in permitting you to continue fishing under tough conditions, but they can also save you from a dangerous situation.

Change
of Direction

The normal casting cycle is basically a straight back and forth procedure. Still there will be several occasions when a change of casting direction may have to be made abruptly. A rising fish may, for example, suddenly show several degrees to your right or left and you want to get on target quickly. Or, it may be required by the overhangs of foliage or other physical considerations of the stream.

Although changing directions is not difficult, it should be attempted in easy to handle degree alterations as a starting point.

There are two strong fundamentals underlying our change of direction casts. The first is the realization that a good backcast always prepares us for an easy forward stroke. The second is the awareness that whatever we do with the rod will be reflected a moment later in the flow and direction of the unrolling line.

As a starting point let's say you want to change the direction of your cast a few degrees to the left. Make the pickup and backcast in the usual manner in the same direction you have been casting, allowing the backcast to extend fully to the rear. Then pivot a few degrees at the hips to face you towards the new target and bring the rod forward. The line will have to follow the new path of the rod's forward stroke. You should be right on target.

More radical degree changes may involve some footwork to ease the amount of change. The procedure is essentially the same. The pickup and backcast are again made in the normal manner, in line with the way you have been casting. With the rod at the top of the backcast, turn your feet and body to the new direction of the forward stroke and move the rod towards the chosen site.

Although the pivot of the feet and body simplify radical direction changes, it is possible you will reach a point where you minimize such movements for most situations. Once the backcast is in position where the rod can effectively push it forward, the direction of the forward cast depends entirely on where you direct the rod. The line must follow the path of the moving stick. You'll be able to make a normal backcast. Simply by moving the rod hand in a new direction on the forward cast, you will easily be making whatever directional alterations you require.

The body pivot is recommended as the starting point so the principles underlying such casts can be seen and felt. If your initial corrections are not enough, you can false cast and continue the pivoting movements until you are right in line with where you want the cast to go.

Make pick-up and backcast in ''old'' casting direction.

As backcast straightens pivot to new direction and complete the forward
stroke.

Pick-up
Variations

The usual pick-up of line is a smoothly accelerating motion up and back. If you happen to use a very long line, you normally make a short line hand pull to move the extended line. Then you lift decisively into a strong backcast. Apart from these usual considerations, there are variations that may be of great help to you under different stream circumstances.

Dry fly anglers normally face the current and like to fish their floaters right back to their boots. Either a half roll or a snap pick-up can come in very handy in this instance.

The half roll pick-up is an incomplete roll cast. The execution starts out just like a conventional roll. As the fly drifts back towards you, elevate the rod slowly, tilting it slightly away from the body. When the line loop has formed outside your elbow, push the rod forward. But instead of following all the way through as you would in the normal roll cast, you stop the rod butt angled about 45° above the water. The moving loop picks line, leader and fly off the water. They bounce into the air. At this point you move back into a conventional backcast. This pick-up also works very well with sinking lines. They are extremely difficult to pick out of the water when deeply submerged. Most experienced deep water workers will retrieve the line rather close to their position which will bring the remaining part of the taper close to the surface. Then the half roll pick-up will kick it all into the air to prepare you for another cast.

The snap pick-up will accomplish much the same thing of picking the remaining line, leader and fly off the water prior to a new backcast. As the line drifts towards you, raise the rod to an almost vertical position. Then apply a quick wrist and thumb snap and stop the rod abruptly. A hump or curve forms which moves down the line to pick the leader and fly off the water. At this point you move up and back to a conventional backcast.

The rod hand drives ahead at the start of the half roll pickup.

Around weeds or other obstructions it is important to use a pick-up that moves the fly straight up, rather than dragging it across obstacles where it may hang up. Along with the possible snap pick-up, you might want to use the switch pick-up. This is accomplished by holding the rod slightly above parallel with the water. Then begin to shake the rod slowly but firmly from side to side while elevating the rod arm. Essentially it is an upward zig zag motion. The curves that form will run down the line and lift everything into the air.

Rod is stopped abruptly at this angle. The moving curve will roll down the line and leader.

Line, leader and fly jump into the air. A new backcast can be started.

The snap pick-up moves a curve down the line to kick leader and fly into the air.

Backcast in progress of formation.

The zig-zagging motion of the switch pick-up
will send "S"-like curves down the line to lift it
into the air.

84

Left, line, leader and fly clear the water and backcast begins. *Right,* a new cast can be directed.

Retrieves

After the cast settles on the water you want to be in a position to strike a fish properly. Form the habit early of getting the line under control right away.

Most anglers place the line over the forefinger of the rod holding hand or secure it lightly between thumb and forefinger of the rod holding hand. All retrieves or line manipulations are done behind this grip to assure you will always be in position to respond to a taking fish.

There are a number of retrieve variations depending on how you wish to animate the fly. Perhaps the most widely used retrieve is the stripping retrieve since you can control the length and speed variations of each stripping motion. The recovered line can be dropped to the water or is often coiled in large loose loops. In coiling the loops, the first one that is gathered in goes well back in the hand, the next loop is placed slightly forward. This procedure is continued with each gathered loop. The last is held in place by thumb and forefinger. At the end of the forward cast the line hand releases the tension. This allows the coiled loops to spiral out in an orderly and progressive manner through the guides.

The hand twist is another time-honored and effective retrieve. The line hand grips the line between thumb and forefinger; then you reach forward with the other three fingers and bring the line back into the palm by rotating the wrist. You'll find the hand is again in position to grasp the line with thumb and forefinger. Alternating these movements will build up a neat grouping of small loops in your hand. They will be held in place by thumb and forefinger and be again released to the next cast by playing them out smoothly and orderly.

After cast, secure line between thumb and forefinger or between forefinger and rod grip.

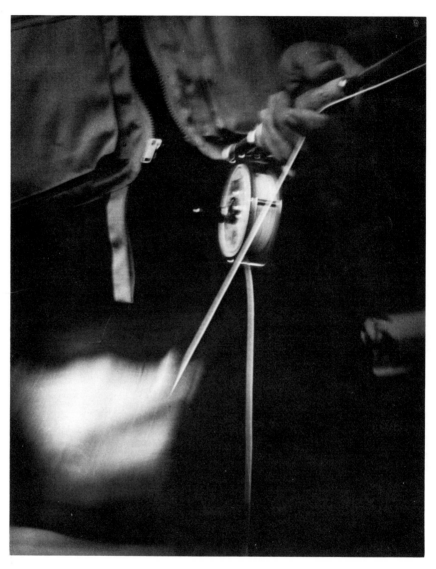

"Blur" shot shows how stripping retrieve is handled. Line is under control should a fish strike.

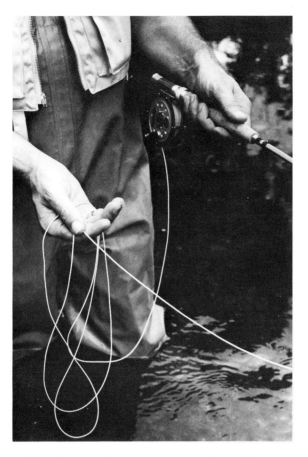

Coiling line is effective method of handling slack.

Hand twist retrieve works fly in slowly.

Flies

With the tremendous scope of modern fly fishing, it would be impractical to do more than hint at the various fly types that may come in for usage. Obviously the types of concern to the individual will be dependent upon the type of fish and the conditions under which they will be sought. If you will be working the salt water, emphasis will be placed on bucktail types simulating the available baitfish species in your area. For some species of sport fish you may wish shrimp imitations also. For others, perhaps surface popping bugs.

The trout fisherman is faced with the greatest variety of fly types available. There are dry flies to simulate the adult insects and nymph patterns suggestive of the immature aquatic insects. The wet fly may suggest partially emerged insects, drowned insects, or they simply may hint of life. The streamer and bucktail concept is baitfish imitation.

For panfish your regular trout patterns will be quite adequate. There are also a number of very effective small poppers which you'll enjoy many a productive outing with.

The black bass angler will have some use for bushy dry fly patterns, some nymphs, wets, and certainly some streamer and bucktail patterns. Furthermore, there are a large number of superb bass bugs and poppers.

The steelhead and salmon anglers depend not so much on the simulation of food forms, but often employ bright attractor types to good advantage.

As a starting point for your particular needs, I would suggest contacting local anglers and reputable dealers for their advice. Their local expertise will help you build a useful collection of types and patterns well-suited to your area needs.

Some fly and popper types.

Knots

There are a number of very fine knots that will in time become favorites. However, as a starting point for the novice fly caster, only a few are required. These are all rather simple to complete and functional for their intended purpose. They are all illustrated here and will do the job.

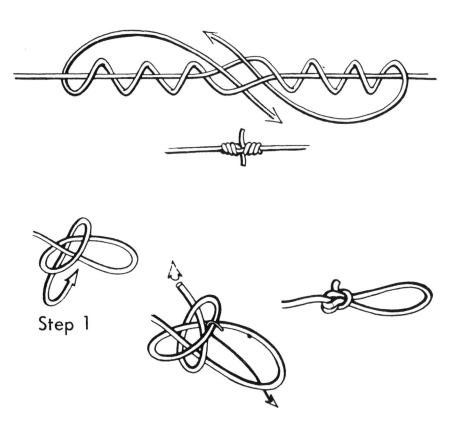

Step 1

1. Put three inches of the end of the line through the leader loop from the bottom side.

LEADER

LINE

2. Pass the end of the line around under the leader loop, then back over the loop, between it and the line where it first came through.

3. Tighten by pulling on line and leader, letting a quarter inch of the end of the line stick out of the knot, and pushing loop and line into snug position with your thumb nail as you gradually tighten them.

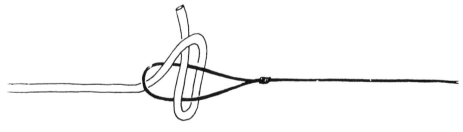

4. Pull hard on line and leader for a few seconds to set the knot.

◀ PULL

PULL ▶

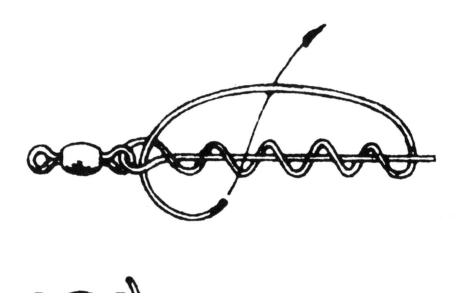

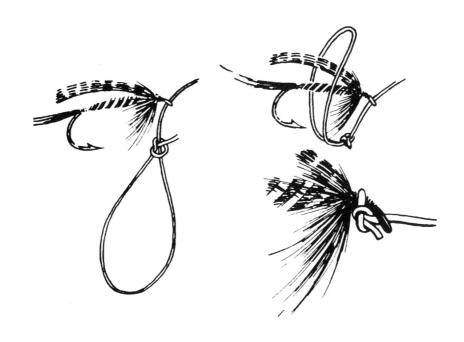

Fly Rods

The novice caster is bound to be confused by the selection of the first fly rod. Even a cursory visit to a well-stocked tackle shop or a short time spent browsing through various catalogs will reveal a tremendous variety of fly rods available. Offerings may range from five feet in length to over nine feet. Various actions may be described, and each rod is touted as being just what is needed. Although the potential for confusion is great, the individual still must come up with a satisfactory starting point . . . *the first fly rod must be pleasant to learn with and functionally suited to the type of fishing you initially anticipate.*

At the risk of oversimplification, we normally find two very common situations existing with beginning fly rodders. The first situation we may term a problem of "all purpose" versatility. For the time being at least, the selected rod will be called on for every task that comes up. Whether the day's outing is stalking panfish on a quiet pond, wading a trout river, or popping a short line with bass bugs. This is the stick that's going along. The requirements are varied to say the least. I suggest consideration of rods in the eight to eight and a half foot lengths using #7 or at most #8 weight lines. Such rods will usually be described as having medium action. While they may be a bit more rod than called for on a small stream with tiny flies or a bit less rod than might be desirable for pushing very bulky, wind resistant bugs or poppers, they do cover this vast middle ground use quite nicely.

The second normal situation arises with the fellow who doesn't require quite as much versatility. His expectations are that he'll primarily be trout fishing the average-sized streams and small ponds.

His day to day problems will center around presentation of trout flies with reasonable accuracy at short to moderate distances of say ten to forty feet. Once in a while he may have to handle a much longer line, but on the whole, accuracy and delicacy are more important than distance. As the best compromise consistent with ease of learning to handle the equipment well, I suggest rods in the seven and a half to eight foot ranges and calibrated to swing a #6 weight fly line. Again, rods of these specifications will usually be described as having a medium action.

At this point it is not worthwhile to delve too deeply into this question of rod action. At best this is boggy ground, for various individuals and tackle firms interpret rod stiffness factors differently. As the most general of guidelines, we find fast, medium and slow often used in describing rod action. Fast indicates a rather stiff, crisp response. Slow indicates a limber, flexible response. Medium action is, of course, in the middle and will assure you of a rod that is neither too stiff or too limber. It is, I believe, the most valid starting point. As your experience grows, you'll be examining this question of rod action on your own. Still, a medium action in modern glass or bamboo from a good maker won't have led you astray.

It is obvious that no single rod can do everything with equal facility, yet that first fly rod introduces you to the sport. If it is too short, too long, too powerful or too heavy, the results can be disastrous. Fly casting will be work, rather than a pleasurable experience.

Perhaps one more cautioning word is in order when we talk about fly rods. Novice hands are often taken in by the apparent appeal of the very light short rods. The first reaction on wiggling say a five or six foot stick is to imagine the thrill of taking a large fish on such a tiny rod. Don't be taken in—at least not yet. Short rods are very demanding of the caster. Faultless timing is needed to make them work well. The bending length is so limited that precision in every stroke is essential. If something goes wrong, say a sagging backcast, it's almost impossible to compensate for. Everything happens too quickly, and every learner will have occasional timing errors that simply add to the problem.

The little sticks are unforgiving. All the equipment factors should help us, rather than hinder us in the learning process.

Consider for just a moment the virtues of starting with the slightly longer rod. When actually fishing, the norm is to be wading the stream or perhaps seated in a boat or canoe. In either case the individual's effective height above the water is reduced. The somewhat longer rod will almost automatically pick up more line, more easily from the water. It will help to hold a higher backcast and, after the cast settles on the water, any mending corrections in the drift of the fly are done more easily with the longer stick.

Later on you may well want to add a fine short rod and light line for those many occasions when such gear is appropriate. But by then you'll be ready for it and can fully appreciate and utilize its special virtues.

The same is true at the other end of the range. If you gravitate toward steelhead, salmon, saltwater or possibly heavy-duty bass bugging where rod power or the need to handle heavy flies under adverse wind conditions may be a factor, you'll instinctively select a long, strong rod and find it most appropriate. Such a rod in the beginning of your casting experience might feel like an arm buster.

Inexperienced anglers hope to find the ideal rod—the one capable of doing every job with equal facility. If there are different fishing requirements there will, in time, be different fishing rods in your collection. There are a number of ideal rods, but no single ideal. The golfer, for instance, couldn't bear the thought of going around the course with but a single club. The need to drive long distances is paramount one moment, a short accurate putt is called for a moment later. The same general problem exists with fly rods. A glassy, smooth surface and a brown trout tipping up to sip in tiny midges is a different ball game than a brown trout lying under the main stream of the Yellowstone and waiting to waylay a sculpin. A bonefish flat is a different world than a steelhead river. Even your favorite stream looks different in April than it will in August. Modern equipment is versatile, but no one outfit is versatile enough for all the conditions that may come up.

Fly Reels

Functionally, the fly reel is the simplest of all reel types. We don't utilize the reel in either casting or retriving the fly.

It stores line and helps us to play large fish. The large fish must be handled off the reel. The small fish can be stripped in by hand, but I believe it is a better practice to get used to using the reel in playing fish. Slack line and a rampaging, heavy fish are a dangerous combination. The slack can catch or hang on the smallest of obstacles.

Another thing the reel doesn't do is aid in the initial strike of the fish. You will gain the habit of retrieving the line over the forefinger of the rod hand to assure an instantaneous reaction to the strike.

So what are you looking for in the average reel? If normal inland work is anticipated, a single action model from a reputable maker will do a fine job. On the average, trout reels may vary from just under three inches in spool diameter to about three and a half inches. Weights will vary from under three ounces to about five ounces. Weight is immaterial within this framework. It is largely an individual preference—some like minimum weight factors, some like the heavier models. There once was a rule of thumb that a reel, loaded with line, should weigh one and a half times the weight of the rod. That may have had some counterweight virtue with the longer, less efficient rods of another era. But today, both power and delicacy are combined into lighter, shorter rods. Also, reel makers combine great strength and durability into light, large capacity reels of modern alloys and aluminum. The more important consideration will be—does the reel have adequate capacity for the type of use we expect? Average fish don't yank off much yardage. If you expect to fish salmon, steelhead or salt water species, you'll want a reel with capacity for 150 yards of twenty pound test Dacron backing. Backing line may be in good order on smaller reels as well, if the fly line doesn't come up to about one quarter to three-eighths of an inch of the crossing braces. Backing will provide a larger arbor for the line to be wound around and will reduce any tendency the fly line may have to take tight "set" coils. The full spool also permits more rapid line recovery, and the backing

Fly Reels: *left to right,* Single Action reel, Single Action reel, Multiplying reel.

is obviously insurance against the occasional heavy fish that makes a marathon move.

Single action reels are, for the most part, interchangeable as to whether you mount the reel handle on the right or left. The normal procedure is to have the reel handle on the right for right handed casters, but there is a growing tendency to "reverse" drag parts and spools so the reel handle is on the left. This means the right handed caster doesn't have to change hands on hooking and beginning to play the fish.

Although virtually all reels feature the handle on the right they do allow for "left-handed" conversion.

There are also automatic fly reels. These are a bit more specialized. They tend to be most popular with panfish and bass fly rodders. Much of this type of work is done from boats. The retrieved line is dropped casually at the anglers feet. Regardless of when the strike occurs during the working of the popper, the slack can be taken up instantly by depressing the trigger. However, there are capacity limitations to automatics, and they do tend to be considerably heavier than single action models of comparable capacities.

The final type in common use is the multiplier. Quietly these have been gaining a following. In salt water as well as on big steelhead, trout and salmon rivers the multi-gearing is ideal. The most popular ratios seem to be $1\frac{2}{5}$ to 1 and 2 to 1. A 2 to 1 ratio simply means that one handle turn brings in two spools of line. If the fish are big and boisterous, you'll gain a quick appreciation of the multiplier and its line recovery capabilities.

The recommended starting point for the average fly fisherman? A quality single action reel that permits interchangeable spools and left handed conversion.

Fly Lines

Today's fly lines are superb. Despite this excellence, several questions arise in line selection. Although it shouldn't be a question any longer, I know from my lecture work that it still is. This is the problem of the line rating systems. Although the industry has adopted a numerical rating since 1961, many still think in terms of the older alphabetical rating system. To clarify this we should review what has happened in the last several years.

Prior to World War II virtually all lines were made of silk. These were labeled by an alphabet system, and the letters were indicative of specific diameters rather than weight. There was a .005 diameter difference between each letter except "H" and "I" where there was a .003 differential. When a combination of letters was used to describe one line, we can see that line incorporated diameter differences, one size tapering to another. Examples would be the HDH double taper designation and say, HCF forward taper.

LINE RATING SYSTEMS

"OLD" Alphabet Letter (By Diameter)

A = .060
B = .055
C = .050
D = .045
E = .040
F = .035
G = .030
H = .025
I = .022

"NEW" Weight Standards

SYMBOLS

L = Level
DT = Double Taper
WF = Weight Forward
ST = Single Taper

WEIGHTS

#	Wt.	Range
1	60	54- 66
2	80	74- 86
3	100	94-106
4	120	114-126
5	140	134-146
6	160	152-168
7	185	177-193
8	210	202-218
9	240	230-250
10	280	270-290
11	330	318-342
12	380	368-392

TYPES

F = Floating
S = Sinking
I = Intermediate (Floats or Sinks)

Weight in grains based on first 30' of line exclusive of any taper tip:

Examples:

DT9S		DT9F	
Tip	←——30 ft. 240 grains	Tip	←——30 ft. 240 grains

(Note: 437½ grains equal 1 ounce)

Since everyone was working with the same basic material, the sizes (based on diameter) worked out nicely. For instance, if one maker's HDH fit your rod, chances are any other HDH would work out satisfactorily.

Then in the late 40's and early 50's companies began applying various synthetics to line making. In a search for superior floating qualities, nylon was utilized; also specialized sinking lines were developed of various materials, particularly dacron. Now we find a critical difference in weight. Nylon is lighter than silk; dacron is heavier. For a time it was entirely possible to select a replacement line for your rod and although it was marked the same as your old silk line, it might have been too light or too heavy for effective casting ease.

The American Fishing Tackle Manufacturers Association in 1961 resolved the problem by changing our rating standards. The result is today's "numbers game." Working on the correct premise that weight is the all important factor in line to rod relationship, diameter of the line is now totally ignored and a weight number identification is used. The unit of weight chosen for the standard is the grain (437½ grains equal one ounce). It was further decided that the average length of the cast was thirty feet; so this system weighs the first thirty feet of line, exclusive of any taper tip. These grain weights range from 60 (No. 1) to 380 (No. 12) plus or minus acceptable manufacturing tolerances. Prefixes were established to designate taper types, "L" for level, "DT" for double taper, "WF" for weight forward and "ST" for single taper. Letters also indicate what the line does (i.e. "F" for floater, "S" for sinker and "I" for intermediate, which like the old silk lines has a specific gravity about that of water). Properly cleaned and dressed, it will float; otherwise it will sink slowly. A typical description then might be DT7F indicating a double taper line of 185 grain which floats, WF7S, a weight forward line of 185 which sinks.

This system greatly simplifies line weight selection. Regardless of taper type and function, any line marked with a specific number conforms to prescribed weight standards. The consumer will find modern rods marked with the proper line weight recommendation and can purchase that recommended line weight with confidence, regardless of whether the line is a floating type, a sinking type, a double taper or a weight forward.

The two most popular designs are the double taper and the weight forward. Both have their virtues. To some extent the choice may be made by considering the type of fishing to be done most often. For example, the double taper is reversible, whereas the weight forward is not. Yet, the weight forward will enable long casts to be made more easily than with the double taper. The double taper presents a fly well at short and medium distances; so too does a well-designed weight forward. By implication then, if you anticipate the line will be used primarily on small streams where delicacy of presentation is the prime consideration and long cast will be the exception to the rule, the double taper is an excellent choice as it is more economical. As one end wears out, the line can be reversed. If the line will be asked to do a variety of jobs or you want to use it on larger water with longer casts, a well-designed weight forward will be more versatile.

The first flyline should be of the floating type. It will be most useful for the most conditions. After that I'm sure you will want to consider a line which sinks in part or in total. Examples of these special types are the so called Sinktip—the first ten feet near the fly are coated to sink, the balance of the line floats, WetHead—the first thirty feet of line near the fly are coated to sink, the balance of the running line will float, or the true Sinking line. As a very broad generalization, average-sized streams and most Atlantic Salmon waters lend themselves to the Sinktip. Deeper, more turbulent rivers, or deep lakes require the WetHead or true sinking line for best results.

The Leader

The leader serves multiple functions. It is a relatively invisible connection between the bulky fly line and the fly. The leader helps in the proper delivery and presentation of the fly, and its suppleness will finally allow the fly to drift on or under the water in a lifelike manner.

The leader is in effect the continuation of the fly line's front taper. We have seen graphically how the belly of the fly line rides forward while the front taper of the line, the leader and the fly lag along during most of the casting cycle and how the energy we've given to the cast must be transmitted through the front taper of the line and leader to extend it fully and drop it all gently. The taper graduation of the leader will determine its effectiveness in achieving these results. The length and possible strength of the leader are concerns of the actual fishing conditions.

As a generalization we find three leader lengths—seven and a half feet, nine feet, and twelve feet—most commonly available.

The shorter leaders such as the 7½ foot length are useful when streams are high or discolored. There is no particular need for the potential deception offered by a longer length. The cloudy water conditions inhibit the ability of the fish to see as well as under more normal circumstances. Also, on small brushy flows where there will be little flyline weight out beyond the rod tip, a short, fast-tapered leader will do an excellent job. Most sinking line work in strong flow is with a short leader, since longer lengths tend to be buoyed towards the surface by the strong flows. To be truly effective under such conditions we want the fly to be digging deep. Duncan Barnes and I were on British Columbia's Dean River a few years back. Our guide had dropped me off at a strong deep flow and had taken Duncan on upriver. The guide got back to me in about an hour. I hadn't had a strike yet. The guide's next question was, "How many times have you been hung on the bottom?" I answered, "None." "That's your answer. These fish won't come up in this kind of water, you've got to go down to them."

Changing to a shorter leader finally helped keep the fly deep. The first steelhead was a strong 10 pounder.

Another area where the short leader is often used is bass bugging around heavy growth. Bass don't tend to be leader shy, and short stout leaders do a fine job.

If there is a normal leader length, I would say it is the nine footer. Average clear water conditions and average casting lengths of say ten to forty feet are ideal for the nine foot choice.

The twelve foot models are favored under difficult, low water conditions, as they do offer the advantage of keeping the bulky fly line end well away from the fly. This permits a gentle delivery of the fly to critical fish in difficult circumstances.

Both knotless and knotted taper will be found in most shops. The knotted leader has, perhaps, always been the standard for comparison. The reason being that the leader maker can exercise total control over strand length and taper graduation. The modern knotless leader is vastly improved, and I do use both types. If there are many weeds or algae in the water, the knotless taper will be more practical. The debris can and will cling to the knots of the knotted taper.

There is one further relationship of importance. That is the fly size to tippet size in use. Without a harmonious relationship here, casting and presentation problems may occur when trying to deliver the fly. As a rule small flies call for light tippets, large flies for correspondingly heavier trippets. The following chart is a valid starting point for your use.

TIPPET SIZE	BALANCING HOOK SIZES
0X	2-1/0
1X	4-6-8
2X	6-8-10
3X	10-12-14
4X	12-14-16
5X	14-16-18
6X	16-18-20-22
7X	22-24-28

By now it is apparent that no single leader length or strength is versatile enough to do it all. There will be changing seasonal and regional needs; so a variety of tapers and strengths is indicated for most of us.

Tying in with this are a couple of further observations. Monofilament tends to retain the tight packaging coils; these should be stretched out before use. Many anglers carry a small square of soft rubber or leather. Drawing the leader, under tension, through the folded square will remove the "memory" coils and permit the leader to lay straight on the water.

Extra tippet spools in the sizes you most often employ will provide a great deal of mileage from a single leader as the tippet strand is the only one which comes in for change.

If you do carry a variety of leaders in your vest, an inexpensive Leader Wallet will be handy. There are compartments to separate the lengths and strengths you use.